Keep Calm & Carry
PEPPER
SPRAY

Strategies, Tactics, & Techniques

for

Personal Safety & Self-Defense

By **Joe Rosner**

Best Defense USA

www.BestDefenseUSA.com

PO Box 129

Hebron, IL 60034

888 439-1411

Table of Contents

Warning!!!
Stop and Read This Before Continuing!

The author, publisher and all other parties involved in the creation, publishing and distribution of this instructional book are not responsible in any manner whatsoever for any injury, harm or loss caused by the application or use of any of the information and instructions included in this work. This includes but is not limited to any and all physical injuries, emotional stress or trauma, loss of property or negative outcome resulting from the methods and practices recommended in this book or by the failure of these methods and practices to protect any person from harm.

Readers must carefully consider their emotional, temperamental and physical characteristics and limitations and use their best, considered judgement before proceeding to teach and apply the methods and practices provided in this book. In the event that any doubt, whatsoever, exists regarding the suitability of any part of this book ERR on the side of caution.

Any reading or use of this book constitutes a Waiver of Liability to author, publisher and all other parties involved in the creation, publishing and distribution of this instructional book.

Warning!!!
Stop and Read This Before Continuing!

Introduction

A re you obsessed with violence? (Am I for writing this book?) After all, chances are much greater you'll die from a stroke, heart disease, cancer or car accident than violence. Yet, even if the probabilities are extremely low, doesn't being prepared to defend yourself and your loved ones from violence that can result in unspeakable suffering, just make sense? Especially since the time, effort, and cost are minor.

What are the chances you will be the victim of a violent crime? It's impossible to say with any certainty. Your age, gender, where you live, work and travel, occupation, race, alcohol consumption practices, even your income, all are factors that can raise or lower your odds of being a victim of violence. Still, the truth is whether the odds are one in five or one in five million, if you're the "one" the odds don't matter. There is another truth: You can refuse to be a statistic.

There are many ways you could choose to reduce your chances of being victimized. Build a castle and never leave it. Learn martial arts. Carry a gun. Get a big, mean dog. All of these have value and all of these have shortcomings. Never leaving your castle is not practical for most people. Martial arts can be effective if you train a lot. But martial arts don't work reliably against armed assailants. Guns? Maybe if you train a lot and are always ready to take a human life on short, one second or less, notice, with no "undo" option. Dogs are great. But most guard dogs are not good family pets.

On the other hand, self-defense spray offers a reasonable level of protection. Self-defense spray does not require strength, athletic ability or constant training. If you make a mistake you're not going to kill someone. Like any tool, you will get better, more reliable results if you take the time to learn how and when to use it. Since you chose to read this book, you probably want to learn how to protect your home, family and friends with self-defense spray.

What Will You Learn from This Book?

- ✓ The different types of self-defense sprays and their pros and cons.
- ✓ How to recognize and avoid dangerous people and situations.
- ✓ Strategies, tactic and techniques for defending yourself and others against single attackers, multiple attackers and animals.

Top 10 Reasons to Carry Pepper Spray

1. It's small, light weight and easy to carry.

2. Extensive training, strength or abilities aren't needed.

3. You can keep some distance from your attacker.

   (It is almost always better to be further away from a potentially violent person.)

4. It is effective on multiple attackers.

5. You'll be less hesitant to use it because it's non-lethal and rarely causes permanent harm.

   (Would you really want to kill or injure a mentally ill person or an acquaintance who is impaired?)

6. It's safer to have around children than a gun.

7. It protects against aggressive dogs and other animals.

8. Fewer legal issues than firearms.

9. If taken and used against you, you are still protected from sexual assault and it is unlikely you be placed in a vehicle.

10. It is inexpensive.

viii | Joe Rosner

FULL DISCLOSURE: There is no one "best defense" for all people and all situations. The average person may be unable or unwilling to devote a great deal of time and money mastering self defense techniques and acquiring hardware. Carrying pepper spray and learning basic strategies, tactics and techniques is, in my humble opinion, the best defense against violence for most people.

Also, the reader should know, the author has professional relationship with ZARC, Inc., the manufacture of VEXOR and CAP-STUN pepper sprays.

ZARC is one of many fine manufactures of pepper spray defense products. Individual readers should be diligent in selecting pepper spray products for their own use.

CHAPTER ONE

History of Aerosol Self Defense

Humans were not the first to defend themselves from an attacker with a noxious gas or irritating spray. Skunks spray a powerful mixture of sulfurous chemicals, called thiols. Accurate up to 10 feet, a skunk's spray is highly-offensive, nauseating to smell, and strong enough to ward off dogs, bears and other potential attackers. Besides the stench it contains a strong irritant and may even cause temporary blindness. Bombardier beetles defend themselves shooting a hot (212 degrees Fahrenheit!), noxious chemical spray from the tip of their abdomen with a popping sound. It is strong enough to kill other insects. Many species of millipedes are capable of producing irritating fluids that may cause allergic reactions. Some millipedes produce defensive sprays containing hydrochloric acid, which chemically burn skin and eyes.

Humans have used chemicals for self-defense for hundreds of years at the very least. Ancient Chinese and Japanese ground cayenne peppers into a fine powder which was either blown in to a target's face or wrapped in paper and tossed at them. This allowed the user to either run away or provided an opportunity to finish off the enemy.

Before World War One chemical weapons were considered "uncivilized" and were outlawed by the Hague Convention of 1899. Yet, within a month of the war's onset, first the French then the Germans were using tear gas (xylyl bromide). The use of non-lethal tear gas led to the use of poison gas intended to kill or result in serious injury.

Tear gas irritates mucous membranes in the eyes, nose, mouth and lungs, and causes crying, sneezing, coughing, difficulty breathing, pain in the eyes, and temporary blindness, typically within 30 to 60 seconds of application. Several treaties outlaw its use in war, but it has and continues to be used for riot control, suppression of protesters and as an alternative to more lethal weapons by law enforcement. Tear gas does not work as well on animals as it does on humans who have a much greater number of tear ducts.

CN and CS gases are the best known types of tear gas, but there are at least 15 types of tear gas that have been developed. CS gas has been experienced as a routine part of training by American soldiers. It is considered non-lethal but there have been credible reports of CS as a factor or cause of death in high doses.

In the 1920s police in France were the first to use less than lethal chemical agents on civilians to quell riots in Paris. In the 1930s chemists began research into the use of oleoresin capsicum as an inflammatory agent for self-defense. (Aerosol Subject Restraint Course Student Manual, 1999 by the New York State Division of Criminal Justice Services.)

MACE, originally known as "Chemical Mace" has become the generic term for all self defense sprays. But like "Kleenex" it is a trademarked product name. Allan Lee Litman invented it in 1965 after a friend of his wife was attacked on the street. The rights to the name and formula has been sold to a number of different companies including Smith and Wesson but is now manufactured by Mace
Security International who make many safety/security products including "The Club" steering wheel lock. The original formula is no longer used but has been replaced by pepper spray or OC. Mace Security International still makes a "Triple Action Spray" that include CS, CN and OC spray.

Pepper spray was first developed as a dog repellent and was adopted by mail carriers in the 1960s. In 1978 Kamran

Loghman invented weapons grade pepper spray technology for law enforcement applications. The FBI approved it in the early 1980s and by 1991 that more than 3,000 local law enforcement agencies were armed with OC. Zarc International offered the first pepper spray, called CAP-STUN, for sale starting in about 1982

The FBI Pepper Spray Scandal

Special Agent Thomas W.W. Ward, a veteran FBI agent pleaded guilty in February 1996 to taking $57,500 from a pepper spray manufacturer in exchange for promoting their product for use by the bureau. Ward was in charge of the Bureau's Less Than Lethal Weapons Program, which researched and tested various chemical weapons.

Ward's duties including making recommendations about the various products. Based on his recommendations, the FBI began purchasing an aerosol product called Cap-Stun. A subsequent investigation found that Ward was receiving money from the company after the FBI approved a purchasing contract.

There have been attempts to use this scandal to discredit pepper spray in general and the Cap-Stun products in particular. However, there has been no research that disputes the effectiveness of OC products and Cap-Stun has changed ownership and continues to provide the FBI and other agencies with pepper spray products.

CHAPTER TWO

What is Pepper Spray?

Pepper spray is not MACE, or tear gas, or CS or CN and there are some real important differences in the effectiveness and properties of these formulations. Although many people, including most news reporters, use these names interchangeably. MACE and tear gases (CN and CS are types of tear gas) are chemical irritants. These manmade chemicals cause pain to the eyes, nose, throat, and lung tissues. Significant production of tears and mucus also occurs. A major shortcoming of all these irritant products is that they are not effective on people if they are drunk, agitated, high on drugs, mentally ill or just have a high pain threshold. Even worse, a certain percentage of the population responds to pain by becoming even angrier and experience a strong adrenaline fueled reaction. The result is a madder, stronger attacker, just the opposite of the intended effect.

In contrast, pepper spray is an inflammatory agent. It will cause an attacker's eyes to swell shut. There have been reports of some people holding their eyes open with their fingers, but their hand cannot be used to press

| 5

an attack. This temporary loss of vision often causes fear and disorientation. Swelling of mucus membranes in the nose and bronchial passages, usually accompanied by spasmodic coughing, reduce the subject's ability to breathe in enough oxygen to continue an attack.

In addition to spasmodic coughing, choking and temporary loss of vision pepper spray will cause pain ranging from mild to severe. The sensation of hotness results from capsaicin binding directly to the pain and heat sensing neurons in the nervous systems of mammals. But these receptors are not in birds or reptiles. Capsaicins activate these neurons creating a strong sensation of heat even when the actual skin temperature is low. Besides the intense burning pain, swelling, redness, occasionally blistering of the skin may result.

000Pepper spray is also known as oleoresin capsicum, OC or capsicum spray when it is intended for use on humans. When it is intended for stopping bears and dog attacks it is called bear spray or HALT, respectively. Popular brands include VEXOR, Sabre, MACE, Bodyguard, Streetwise and Fox Labs.

The active ingredient in pepper spray is capsicum, which is a chemical distilled from the same hot peppers you may enjoy eating. Hot and sweet peppers are part of the

Wilbur Scoville who devised the Scoville Organoleptic Test

capsicum genus, which includes the mild, inoffensive bell peppers, chili peppers, jalapenos, habaneros, cayenne and many more. It is estimated 50,000 capsicum varieties are grown around the world.

The "hotness" of peppers and OC formulations is commonly rated in Scoville Heat Units or SHUs.

000Common Scoville Heat Unit Ratings

Professional Grade OC	**15 Million**
Consumer Grade OC	**2 Million**
Ghost Pepper	**200,000**
Habanero	**100,000**
Jalpeno	**2500**
Bell Pepper	**0**

Extraction of oleoresin capsicum from peppers requires capsicum to be pulverized and then mixed with an organic solvent like ethanol. After filtration, the solvent evaporates leaving a wax-like resin, which is oleoresin capsicum.

If the product is to be used in a spray, the oleoresin capsicum is mixed with a liquid so that it can be sprayed. Different brands of OC spray may be mixed with water, alcohol, or organic solvents. Some products use a dry form of OC and either blast it out of a gun-type device or use it to fill a projectile ball that bursts upon impact.

The liquid OC is added into a dispenser can along with a propellant. Common propellants used to pressurize the contents include nitrogen, carbon dioxide, ohalogenated hydrocarbons, including Freon, tetrachloroethylene, and methylene chloride.

How Effective is Pepper Spray?

There is no single self-defense method that is 100% reliable and 100% risk free, but pepper spray does come close. One study *(The Effectiveness and Safety of Pepper Spray, Office of Justice Programs, National Institute of Justice),* found OC spray successfully incapacitated humans in 156 out of 174 (90%) confrontations when deployed by police. Even when a person is not completely incapacitated by a dose of OC their ability to commit violence will be downgraded. A 1999 study of 690 incidents of pepper spray use by law enforcement (*Robert J.Kaminski,* Steven M. Edwards, and James W. Johnson, "Assessing the Incapacitative Effects of Pepper Spray During Resistive Encounters With Police,"

Policing: An International Journal of Police Strategies and Management) found pepper spray was effective 85% of the time, according to the broadest definition of the term "effectiveness."

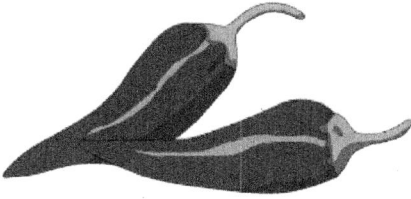

There are many factors that can impact how effective OC spray is in stopping aggressive behaviors. These include but are not limited to:

- Previous OC exposures

- Distance to/from subject

- Strength of OC formulation

- Targets use of masks, goggles and/or protective clothing.

- Meteorological conditions

- Subject's health

Nobody is immune to the effects of being exposed to pepper spray. However, being exposed to an OC application one or more times can allow an individual to build up tolerance to its effects. In fact, it is a fairly common practice for police agencies to spray officers undergoing OC training and then require them to perform a task such as a weapons retention drill. Results of this training show that officers can learn to remain "goal focused," and can become less sensitive to the pain caused by the OC. There is also at least some anecdotal evidence that individuals who consume very spicy food regularly are more likely to experience milder effects.

Most civilian pepper spray encounters occur at about a four-foot range, well within the effect range of most pepper spray dispensers. However, the further the distance from canister to target the more dispersed the liquid OC will be and the less will land on the attacker's face. Therefore, it is important to know the specific distance the product is intended to cover and stay within that range. If an OC spray is stored in a cold location, such as a vehicle in cold weather, expect that effective spray range will be reduced.

Weather conditions impact how quickly and how well pepper spray is working in stopping violence. The warmer the temperature, the better it works. Humidity is believed by many to make the pepper spray take effect faster. Rain and wind can make it harder to spray a target as they can effectively disperse the spray. Many people worry that if they need to spray someone up wind from them the spray may blow back and incapacitate them. But, since most pepper spray encounters happen at about a four foot distance, and because pepper spray must be applied to the eyes and face for maximum incapacitation, this is usually not an issue.

How Safe is Pepper Spray?

A 1999 study of nearly 700 cases of pepper spray use by law enforcement found pepper spray was effective 85 percent of the time and that none of the people arrested in these incidents died in custody. There have been some reports of people with underlying health issues and/or taking certain street drugs dying after being sprayed with OC.

Use of alcohol as the liquid carrier or flammable propellants has been a concern. The TV show Mythbusters showed two out of five canisters they tested by spraying through a six inch flame did project flames out two to four feet. Two incidents in which the subject caught fire when sprayed with OC were found after extensive Internet searches. In one case a soccer fan was sprayed with an unknown product resulting in bright fire of short duration. In another instance, a man's hair caught fire when police Tasered him at the same time as was sprayed. However, police indicated his hair may have contained a 0011flammable substance, either a hair oil or paint thinner.

TIP: *Is wasp spray better than pepper spray for self-defense?* Many Internet "experts" claim it is. But the facts don't support this. Wasp spray can cause serious harm to people but will be too slow acting to protect you. Also, intentional use, especially if planned ahead, can get you in legal trouble. So yes, as a last resort use bug killer. But it should not a first choice.

CHAPTER THREE

Choosing a Pepper Spray That Meets Your Needs

You wouldn't use a screwdriver to hammer a nail, would you? Pepper spray is a tool, and like any other tool should be matched to the job. Considerations include size, ease of aiming effectively, spray pattern, strength and quality of manufacture. There are also OC products for special situations like inside buildings.

A fire extinguisher-sized sprayer (bear spray) that shoots a lot of liquid pepper 20 plus feet provides great firepower. But, is it practical to carry around? A tiny OC dispenser the size of an AAAA battery is easy to carry but is very limited on range and capacity.

Personal, keychain units, that hold about a half-ounce of liquid OC, are generally the best choice to carry on a regular basis. There are several manufacturers who use the same hard-shell ½ ounce case, so you cannot judge a pepper spray by its looks. Read the label and do your research. Many hard-shell, ½ ounce units include a built-in belt clip.

The most common personal keychain pepper spray units have a trigger that swivels to the side to place it in the safe mode. Turning it back to the center makes it ready to "fire." This style of dispenser is unlikely to go of in your purse or pocket. You can depress trigger with your index finger, or with your thumb. Using your thumb give you a better grip, making it easier to keep hold if an assailant attempts to grab it away from you. Plus, you can use the hardcase as a striking tool. At the same time, pressing when the trigger with your thumb, it is vital that your top finger not block the nozzle. A newer model personal pepper spray unit uses a flip top safety and has a small protruding lip that helps ensure your fingers remain clear of the nozzle.

Pepper spray canisters that hold two or more ounces are good choices for your home, business or vehicle and for those who plan on keeping it in a holster.

Pepper sprays disguised as pens or lipsticks have the advantage of being able to hide in plain sight. However, the three steps of removing the cap, aiming and then pushing the top down to fire make them slower to use in ambush type situations. Also, you will need to look at it, instead of at the assailant, to be sure you're aiming correctly. While these are not recommended for regular carrying situations they may be a good choice if you anticipate being a victim of domestic or acquaintance violence.

> **TIP:** Pepper sprays that come in soft, leatherette holsters with snaps are not recommended as it takes too long to unsnap the top, turn the trigger, aim and fire. It is also very likely that the holster's top strap will flop around and interfere with the spray,

If you can't put product on target your pepper spray is useless. Two important factors in selecting a spray that aims easily and accurately are ergonomics and pattern. A well thought out ergonomic design helps you intuitively grip the unit in a way that helps you aim it. General Equipment Corporation's Spitfire aims at wherever your thumb is pointed. Most canister and keychain type dispensers naturally fit in your hand so that, much like any other aerosol, it will spray where your pointer finger is aimed.

There are three common spray patterns of pepper spray. A stream pattern shoots the furthest and is the most windproof. It also requires an exact aim that is difficult in dark or low vision situations. A fog pattern has a much more limited distance and is more impacted by wind, but requires little in the way of aiming. The third pattern is the cone, which combines the best aspects of the other two types.

The major factors effecting the strength or effectiveness of a pepper spray are Scoville Heat Units and percentage of OC. There is no agreed upon, objective standard that determines the relationship between how hot and effective a spray is. Variables include the sobriety level of the suspect. Is he stoned, drunk, enraged, or mentally ill? People respond to OC and to pain differently. Some shut down, but some become enraged. Previous exposures, alcohol and drug use, etc., all are factors.

Pharmacist Wilbur Scoville his the Scoville Organoleptic Test in 1912 to measure the pungency (hotness) of various spices. Bell peppers are rate at zero SHUs, jalapenos at 1500 to 4500, habaneros are rated at up to 100,000 ShUs, and a ghost pepper can hit one million. To find the SHU, a measured amount of ground, dried pepper is diluted with sugar water. Panels of three or more people sample the solution until a level of dilution is found where the heat from the pepper can no longer be detected. The diluted the mix of dried pepper to sugar waters the higher the SHU. Pure capsicum is between 15 and 16 million SHUs. You would have to dilute up to 16 million times before it could no longer be detected.

Percentage of capsaicinoids is determined by testing the amount of capsaicinoids in a batch of known size using a high performance liquid chromatography (HPLC). There are six different capsaicinoids: Capsaicin, Pelargonylvanillylamide, Dihydrocapsaicin, Ordihydrocapsaicin, Homodihydrocapsaicin, and Homocapsaicin. But the "majors", Capsaicin and Pelargonylvanillylamide are anywhere between 25% to 400% stronger than the other four. Pepper spray is produced from the fruit of pepper plants. The amount of capsaicinoids in a plant will vary, a lot, depending on the nutrients present in the soil, amount of sunshine, etc. So a higher percentage of Capsaicin and/or Pelargonylvanillylamide is most desirable.

Nozzle heat is the percentage of capsaicinoids times the SHUs. If you multiply 15 million SHUs times 1% you get 150,000 Out The Nozzle SHUs. So, why not make 20, 30 or 50 percent OC spray? At a concentration stronger than about 10% the capsaicinoids tend not to atomize well, resulting in a clumpy, less effective spray.

Is pepper spray one hundred percent effective? No, but what is? There's no shortage of videos on the Internet showing police and military being sprayed with pepper spray. They usually are required to complete a number of tasks such as answering questions, punching a bag or running. How effective is pepper spray if someone can be sprayed with it and still do that kind of stuff? But notice how the spray is applied after the recipient is told to close their eyes and mouths? Even people who can withstand the burning pain will have their ability to commit violence greatly degraded.

> TIP: OC spray confidence builder. You do not need to be sprayed directly with OC to understand its effectiveness. Spray a small amount into a jar with a screw-on lid. You can test strength of the spray and your reaction to it by holding your face near the jar and inhaling very slightly. Another test is to wet a cotton swab with pepper spray and apply to your cheek an inch or more below your eyes.

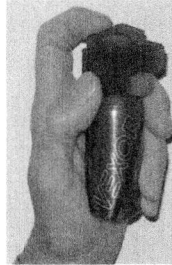

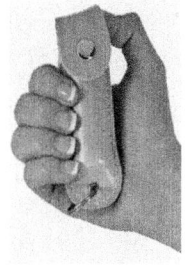

Keychain, Canister and Leatherette Holster (Not recommended.)

So what's your best choice? Here's a checklist of important features-

- ✓ Easy to carry with you
- ✓ Positive safety that will not fire in your purse or pocket
- ✓ Child resistant, if you're around kids
- ✓ Easy, "no look", deployment and aiming

✓ Effective nozzle heat of 100,000 or better

There is no single best pepper spray product for all people and situations. For most people, the best strategy may be carrying a half-ounce, hard-shell spray on their keychain and keeping a two-ounce canister at home, at the office and in their vehicle.

> **TIP:** When it comes to Concealed Carrying of Firearms (CCW) both sides have merit. Well trained, law abiding, responsible citizens arming himself or herself makes everyone safer. The two issues of concern are; Not everyone is a good candidate for CCW; and the training requirements are not nearly adequate. Should you decide to get a CCW card take additional training from a qualified instructor.
>
> Carry a weapon AND pepper spray provides a less than lethal option. Which is useful as not all crimes are capitol offenses.

CHAPTER FOUR

Self Defense Concepts

Because there is no guarantee that any self-defense weapon or use of self-defense will always work in every situation, it is better to avoid confrontations that require using your pepper spray than to use it. Black belts lose fights and police officers sometimes do, too. You will never lose a fight that you avoided in the first place.

Be aware! Be very aware!

Whether you're carrying pepper spray or not, you can keep yourself safer by making good decisions. You can make good decisions by planning ahead. You can make good plans by getting good information. Experts agree, having a plan in advance is the best way to minimize your chances of being victimized. Think about what you may need to do in response to a threat BEFORE you need to do it. How will you get there and back? So let's first review ways to avoid dangerous people and situations. Awareness can be broken down into two types: strategic and situational.

Strategic awareness is the information you can get ahead of time to review the risk of finding yourself in a threatening situation and to take steps to manage that risk.

Look around for men and ask yourself,
"Who is he and why is her hereg?"

- Google the phrase "crime map" with the zip code of a location you plan to visit. Chances are good, local law enforcement is posting or mapping crime info online. You can then see what types of crime are happening where and when. Often there will be a description or even a photo of a perpetrator who is committing a crime.

- Check the weather. Hot weather increases the overall likelihood of violent behavior. Colder and wetter weather usually mean fewer people will be out and about. So there'll be fewer people around as witnesses or to help if you're attacked by a stalker.

- Time of day can also be part of your strategic thinking. Going earlier in the morning is better for higher crime risk areas. As mentioned previously, if you're worried about a specific person or persons go when there will be the most people around. If you're partying or working in a nightlife district crime risks go up after midnight.

1. Check news sources to see what events might be in your vicinity. Mardi Gras, large sports events, controversial trials, and college homecoming can all increase your chances of being attacked. Know what events are happening so you can plan to mitigate the risks.

Tactical awareness, also called situational awareness, is gained by gathering and processing information in real time on the spot. Stop! Look! Think! Before getting out of your vehicle, walking to your vehicle, entering a park, getting off a bus or train, look around and assess your situation. Keep your head swiveling, just being alert reduces your chance of being selected as a victim. Ask yourself: *Who's there and why?* "

Keep in mind:

- Men are more likely to commit violence than women.

- Larger or more athletic men are more capable of violence.

- More than one potential assailant increases your risk if attacked.

- Does their clothing fit the weather and location and/or conceal their face?

- What sources of help are available?

1. Are there businesses, schools, homes or offices you can flee to?

2. Within the range of your voice, are there people who may help you

3. Can you hail a passing vehicle if you need help?

4. Are there any call boxes, panic buttons nearby?

5. Is there a security alarm system or fire alarm you can use to alert the authorities?

6. Is your mobile phone charged and ready?

> **TIP:** Think about how to make an effective 911 call BEFORE you need to. The two key elements are the nature of your emergency and the location. For example, *"I'm calling to report an assault in progress, 123 Main Street.")*

1. What are the best escape routes?

Quickly, what is the fastest route to outside from where you're reading right now? Get on the habit of ALWAYS knowing, just like when you board an airliner.

Are there any rooms, vehicles or other spaces where you can securely shelter in place?

CHAPTER FIVE

Carrying Pepper Spray

Where will you carry your pepper spray? You need to be sure you can get it in your hand fast and without looking, so it should not be buried in your purse or the glovebox of your car. It should be secured so that an assailant can't grab it or played with by children. Pepper spray carry options include:

Holsters are best for larger, two ounce and up, canisters. A good quality, properly sized for your canister, holster allows you to draw your OC fast. Make sure it holds the can well enough to prevent it from falling out if running, bending over, etc. The downside of carrying your spray in a holster is the loss of surprise. Everyone will know you have pepper spray.

Belt Clips are built in to many pepper spray dispensers. These can be a good way for joggers, walkers and bicyclists to carry their protection. Make sure your belt or waistband works well with your sprayer so it does not fall off, but at the same time allows for a fast draw. A shirt, jacket or sweater can be used to conceal your pepper spray unit. Some types of belt clips can be used to attach your spray to the sun visor of your car or the brake cable of your bicycle.

> **TIP:** A hard case, keychain-sized pepper spray can be attached to a commonly available silicone bracelet for easy hands free carry.

Pocket carry is an option, too. Make sure you can get your spray out quickly, but at the same time be sure it can't
accidentally fall out. Some pepper sprays, for instance General Security Corporation's "Spitfire" have been known to discharge in pockets, so do exercise caution.

Purse or fanny packs are good carry options, but you must make sure you can find and deploy a pepper spray fast.

Carrying pepper spray in your car provides protection from road-ragers, car-jackers and other assailants. Don't just toss it in the glove box where you may have a hard time finding it quickly. Pepper Shot sells a 1/3 ounce Auto Pepper Spray designed to clip to your visor. In many cars the best place to store your OC is the center console where it is right at hand in an emergency, but not if you leave kids alone in the car. Look under the steering column where many cars have a small storage space perfect for keeping your spray concealed, but within easy reach.

TIP: Most manufacturers do not recommend storing pepper spray in your car if the temperature could exceed 120 Fahrenheit, which can happen on any sunny day when the outside air temperature exceeds 80 degrees. Some brands are more heat tolerant. Kimber Guardian Angel is safe up to 176 Degrees and Vexor up to 150.

The author has carried pepper spray in the center console of various cars for years and never experienced any problem.

Whether you should conceal your pepper spray or brandish it as openly as a warning will depend on the situation. If you're walking a long and you see a man coming towards you, get your spray in hand and ready to fire, but keep it hidden in your pocket. If a person is actively threatening you or others, hold up your spray at the ready and firmly instruct them to keep their distance and yell, **Stay Back!**

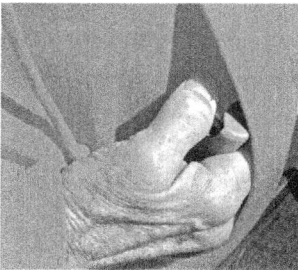

In the pocket.

Ready stance. Yell, *"Back Off!"*

CHAPTER SIX

Defending Yourself with Pepper Spray

S elf-defense situations can develop slowly or suddenly, and without notice. You need to be ready to deal with either. In either case, the earlier you can recognize and react the better your chances of a good outcome.

Be prepared, not scared!

Sudden attacks, by definition, happen with little or no warning. That does not mean you can't be ready. Most sudden attacks will happen in higher risk areas, locations that are isolated and offer places of concealment. Parking lots are high on that list as are jogging trails, stairwells, some ATMs, bus stops or train platforms and buildings that are empty because they're unoccupied or it's after hours. To be ready have your pepper spray in hand with your finger on the trigger ready to spray. If someone runs up behind you or jumps up from concealment you're ready to fire. If you get in the habit of keeping your pepper spray in hand whenever you're in an area with higher risk, you'll be prepared to take action if ambushed.

Many attacks develop slower and at some point you should recognize the growing threat and be ready to act. It is also important to use responsibly and be ready to explain why you felt threatened and why you took the steps you did. Here are some situations to think about.

Scenario 1 - A customer/patient/visitor at work becomes more and more upset. They begin to talk louder, clench their fists and their face starts to redden. You explain you want to help, but that you are not going to be able to fix the issue. At this point they threaten you, act in a threatening manner while getting too close or entering your workspace. For instance, they come behind the counter or into the nursing station.

Do you:

- Spray them with your pepper spray?

- Run away to a safe place and call 911?

- Move a safe distance away, brandish your OC spray and tell them to leave?

Best choices in order are B, C and only if absolutely necessary, A.

Scenario 2 - An acquaintance is dropping you off after a social or business function. They begin making unwanted sexual advances. You try the car door but find it's locked.

Do you:

- Clearly and firmly tell them to stop and warn them of the consequences if they continue?

- Hold your pepper spray in your hand that is furthest away warn them you'll spray them if they don't let you out immediately?

- Spray them in the face and then break the car window with the bottom of your sprayer?

Best choices in order are A, B, C.

Scenario 3 - You're walking across a parking lot after dark. You see an unknown man you think may be following you or seems to be lurking near your car. The parking lot is reasonably well lit, but there are no other people nearby.

Do you:

A. Wait until they get close and ask them what they want while displaying you're pepper spray?

B. Hold your pepper spray in your pocket ready to fire and continue to your car?

C. Go back into the store or office and ask for an escort?

Best choices in order are C, B, A.

Scenario 4 – You are in your car, stopped at a light. A man approaches and motions for you to roll down your window. You cannot tell if he is a panhandler, needs help or is a criminal looking to victimize you.

Do you:

    A. Lower the window all the way and say hi?

    B. Back your car up to get room and then drive away?

    C. Detach your pepper spray from your keys, keep the car running and lower the window just an inch?

Best choices in order are C and B.

Scenario 5 – You're rushing to pick up a few items you need to make dinner. You've had a long hard day. As you wait in the 10 items or less line at the store you see the women in front of you has 14 items.

Do you:

    A. Keep your pepper spray concealed but get it ready. Then tell her she's rude and demand she go to another cash register?

    B. Tell the nearest store employee?

    C. Wait patiently?

Best choices in order are C and A.

Scenario 6 – You're walking on a moderately busy commercial street. A man comes up to you asks for directions or the time.

Do you:

A. Say "Sorry, I can't help you," and just keep walking?

B. Step into a nearby store?

C. Pepper spray him?

D. Turn sideways with dominant side away from him and get your pepper spray in hand, ready to fire, then answer?

Best choices in order are A, B, D and C if needed.

"What if?"

Do you agree or disagree with the answer for the previous scenarios? The truth is only you can decide what to do in any given circumstance. But the time to think about your reaction is <u>BEFORE</u> you need to react. Pilots are taught to always play "What if?" as they fly along. What if, the engine quits? Where can I land this airplane? So that in the unlikely event the motor stops, they already have a plan. No need to think about what to do, just decide to do it. One important reason you want to be in the habit of playing "What if?' is that when a major threat is realized you'll likely get a big dump of adrenaline into your bloodstream. For most people, the first sign is a loss of peripheral vision, accompanied by a loss of fine motor skills and most importantly, you lose the ability to think clearly. But if you've already imagined "what if", you'll do "if" and be ready to react effectively.

How to Use Your OC Spray "IF"

BE READY! When out walking, keep your OC spray in your hand, clipped to your belt, or in a pocket which can be easily and quickly reached with your dominant had. Whenever you sense a potential threat position your hand on your spray ready to fire. REMEMBER TO SWITCH THE OC SPRAY'S TRIGGER BACK TO "SAFE" IF MOVED TO THE "FIRE" POSITION!

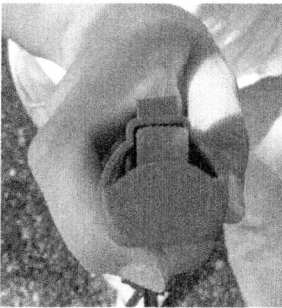

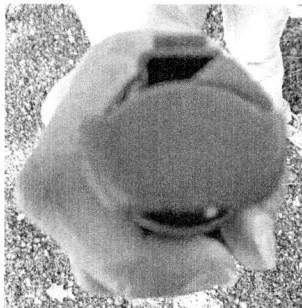

Safety Off Ready to Fire   Safety On Can't Fire

When driving you may decide to carry a pepper spray for protection. (Either a keychain unit attached to your key ring or a canister in the center console or other easy to reach location.) In order to avoid ever needing your spray practice the following safe driving techniques:

Always lock your doors and start the car immediately upon entering. Fasten your seat belt, put your phone in its holder, look at your receipts, and buckle in the kids only AFTER the doors are secured and the motor is started.

In traffic or at a stoplight, leave enough space between your car and the one in front so you can maneuver and drive away.

Road rage is a dangerous and stupid response to certain, rude, aggressive or dangerous behaviors another driver engages in. These behaviors stimulate a primitive part of the human mind, known as the "reptilian brain" which consists of the brainstem and cerebellum. Road-rage happens when the reptilian mind feels threatened and responds aggressively as it feels its/your survival is on the line. The rational parts of the mind are no longer in control and a minor incident now turns into a violent encounter. Road rage can be prevented or mitigated by:

1. Keeping control of your own temper.

2. Not reacting to another driver's bad behavior.

3. Practicing good, courteous driving habits.

If you find yourself being threatened by an aggressive driver, ignore verbal abuse and rude gestures. Do not engage the aggressor. Keep your doors locked and your windows up. Do not stop or get out of the car. If you are being followed, call 911, head to the nearest police station or any other public place where there is help.

If you try to use pepper spray through the window of a stopped or moving vehicle it may blow back into your face. The only time to use pepper spray inside a vehicle is if the attacker is also in the car.

If you think you're being followed, make three left turns. If the vehicle of concern is still behind you, you're being followed. Immediately call 911 and drive to the nearest police station or other safe location. Don't stop and confront the other driver!

AIM! The aiming point for pepper spray is the center of the face. Maximum results are obtained when the assailant's eyes are swollen shut due to the inflammatory effect of the spray and the bronchial passages are inflamed enough to cause spasmodic coughing.   Spraying   an attacker on the chest, hands, etc. will not be effective in stopping an attack. Some people are able to withstand the pain and continue to function. However, the temporary blindness caused by the direct application of OC to the eyes greatly reduces their ability to find their victim and launch an effective attack. When pepper spray droplets contact the bronchial passages the intense coughing makes it very difficult to breathe in enough air to maintain a sustained physical attack. In addition, the involuntary, spasmodic coughing reduces their ability to concentrate and focus.

OC Defense While Standing

Stand "bladed" by turning sideways to the aggressor. Your dominant hand holds the OC (find ON trigger ready to shoot) and is extended out about 3/4 of a full extension. Position your non-dominant, rearward hand, about half way between your head and the dominant, forward, shoulder. Keep the rear hand open. Its job is to protect your face and throat. Your feet are slightly wider than your shoulders. Attempt to keep as much distance between you as practical.

This self-defense position-

> is non-aggressive and less likely to exacerbate a situation.

> provides the narrowest target.

> makes it hard for someone to push you down.

> allows you to quickly pivot on your front foot to keep the OC between you and an attacker.

> lets you move away with a "sliding side step" knowing you're unlikely to trip or slip.

> positions you to easily pivot on the balls of your feet and run away.

If you know you're under attack, or about to be under attack, shout *"Back Off!" "Stay Away!," or "Help! I'm being attacked! Call 911!"*

0If the situation has not yet become violent or extremely threatening, you may attempt to de-escalate it with phrases like: *"I'm sorry. I don't want to fight. I'm not looking for trouble."* and then walk or run away.

> **TIP: The Bystander Effect** Should you yell "Fire" instead of help? Probably not. Many people, including some crime prevention instructors believe yelling "fire" is best. The phenomenon of not helping when others are being harmed is called the "Bystander Effect". The bystander effect is a social psychological phenomenon where individuals do not offer any means of help to a victim when others are present. It is often true the greater the number of bystanders, the less likely any individual will help. they all assume someone else will step up and help. The formula for breaking through the bystander effect is attention, problem, solution. For example: ***"Help! I'm being attacked! Call 911!*** Even better, point out an individual bystander and ask them to get involved. ***"You in the blue shirt! Help! I'm being attacked! Call 911!"***

If a person is clearly ready to hurt you, point the pepper spray at their face and push HARD on the trigger for 1/2 to one full second. Step back and to one side several steps, staying in your stance, and observe whether or not it is safe for you to move to a safe location and call for help. Be prepared to fire again if required.

As soon as you spray, move away! An attacker who is temporarily blinded may still try grabbing you. Move quietly and keep your distance. Step back and to one side if possible.

Be ready to spray an attacker more than once, if necessary.

OC Defense While Seated or Reclined

When most people think about rape, they envision a stranger hiding behind a bush or in a dark alley. The reality is 80% of sexual assaults are committed by an acquaintance. Typically, it's a friend, a current or former boyfriend, or a classmate. Sadly, a large percentage of these sexual assaults are not reported. (Yes, it happens to men, too, but nowhere near as often.) It just makes sense to have your pepper spray nearby and accessible at all times. Some women will attach their sprayers to their bras or elsewhere inside their clothing in order to be sure it is always there if needed.

If your spray is in your purse or jacket and you begin to feel uneasy, make an excuse, like "I want to make sure I didn't lose my keys," and retrieve them.

If your date or friend will not take "No" for an answer, and/or attempts to use force, place the OC sprayer as close to their nose area as you can and push the trigger. At the same time, place your free hand over your own face, covering your eyes, nose and mouth. As quickly as possible get up, get to a safe place and get on the phone to 911.

The OC spray may affect you both. In most cases you will still be able to escape. Remember that while OC spray is extremely unpleasant if it is sprayed near you or on any part other than your face, it generally takes a shot to the face to be disabling.

> **TIP:** If you're getting too drunk or too high you greatly increase your risk of sexual assault or other crimes. This in no way means you deserved to be victimized anymore than leaving a door unlocked means you deserve to burglarized. When you plan to imbibe, having a designating a non-drinker to watch out for everyone else is a good idea, even if you're not driving.

OC Defense Against Multiple Attackers

If you are attacked or threatened by multiple aggressors, perhaps the best tactic is to hold the trigger down while aiming back and forth across the entire group. Or, if the assailants are in front of you spray the closest and/or the instigator. The others may be reluctant to press the attack after seeing one of their comrades in agony.

> **TIP:** If you find yourself facing an n aggressive dog, blade yourself as previously described. Watch the dog without making eye contact. Move away slowly in a sliding side step. If circumstances permit, spraying a small amount of OC between you and the dog may cause it to back off. Be ready to aim for the dog's face if moves in to attack.

OC Defense On the Run

If you are in a situation where you're being chased or are approached from behind by an attacker, bring your canister across the front of your body and spray over your opposite shoulder as you run. Do not try and shoot pepper spray over the shoulder or under the opposite arm.

Self-defense Techniques for Getting to Your OC

What if you're under attack before you know it? Your pepper spray is still in your purse, pocket or desk drawer. The techniques described here should be practiced carefully and with great concern for your practice partner's safety and your own. You may wish to get additional training from a qualified instructor.

Escape from Single Hand Wrist Grab

When an aggressor grabs your wrist, using only a single hand, take these steps:

> Turn your wrist so the narrow, thumb edge of your wrist lines up with the attacker's thumb and forefinger.

> Push your own elbow towards the attacker's knuckles to "lever' your wrist free. Bring your other hand over to help if extra strength is needed.

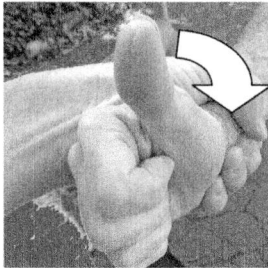

Rotate wrist to thumb and forefinger.

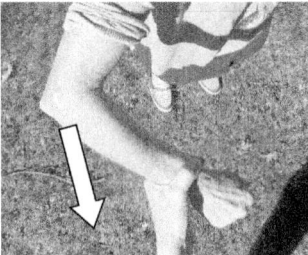

Lever elbow inward.

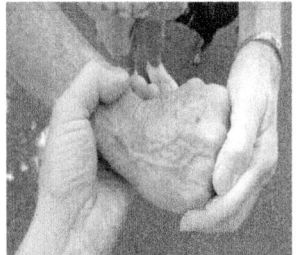

Use your helper hand to pull.

Escape From Two Handed Wrist Grab

Should an assailant grab one or both of your wrists with both of their hands, perform the following actions:

1. Clasp your hands together. If an assailant' two hands on one of your wrists reach over the top to clasp your hand that is being held.

2. Quickly shove down.

3. Step back and pull your hand up by your ears.

Push down hard!

Swing hands to ear and step back.

Always pull to the ear.
Not chest, overhead or face.

Escape from a Choke

If someone has their hands around your throat, from the front or rear, you can escape by:

1. Raising both hands as high up as you can.

2. Simultaneously step back and turn/twist away.

Defense against a front bear hug will depend on whether or not you have an arm free. If yes, grab your spray, aim and fire. If you do not have a free arm, drive one of your knuckles as hard as you can into the attacker's lowest rib.

Punch knuckles into lowest rib.

Defense against a rear bear hug can be done with one of the following methods. Drop your weight down and then spring back up driving the top of your head into the assailant's chin. Stomp on their feet. Or reach back to their groin, grab hard, yank and twist.

Protect yourself against being thrown to the ground by hooking one of your feet behind the opponent's lower calf.

Defense From the Ground

If knocked to the ground you must prepare to defend yourself as fast as possible. If you cannot get back on your feet quickly, sit up, and use your feet and hands to spin about, keeping your feet between yourself and the person of concern. If you can reach your pepper spray hold it up, aim and fire if a clear opportunity is presented.

Combining Self-defense Tactics with OC Spray

When confronting a violent assailant your goal is always to escape, get to a safe location, and call for help. There may be situations where it is not possible to get an accurate, effective shot with your pepper spray or you may encounter an individual with a high pain tolerance that is able to continue to attack you after being sprayed. Nevertheless, almost everyone who is sprayed with OC loses all or most of their vision and their ability to attack is greatly reduced. Running away to safety and help is always best if practicable. But, if circumstances REQUIRE you to ensure the threatening person's ability to continue an attack is eliminated, use the following self defense tactics.

An ideal self defense tactic should be reliably effective, easy to remember and use under stress, not require strength or athleticism and work well, even if not executed to perfection. When self-defense spray is also being used, techniques that avoid getting pepper spray on your face or hands are best.

STOMP KICK: After or simultaneously with spraying your target, position yourself sideways to the assailant and take a sidestep towards them while bringing your nearest knee up high. Slam your foot down on their foot at a 90-degree angle, as close to their ankle as you can. Immediately step back away and to one side.

STEP& PUSH: This technique is very similar to the stomp kick, but used when you need to control somebody yet wish to avoid injuring them. For example, a friend who had too much to drink or a person suffering dementia. Again, slide in with a side step, quickly, but gently, put your foot on top of theirs with enough of your weight to hold it firm. Then give them a firm shove backwards. They will lose their balance and fall on their back.

PASSIVE BLOCKING: Should you find yourself temporarily unable to defend yourself due to being stunned by a blow, panic or an overwhelming "blitz" attack, you'll need to take steps to protect yourself long enough to make a new plan. Use your elbows to form a cage around your face and neck. Shielding will only work for 8 to 10 seconds. But that is enough time to grab and deploy your pepper spray.

Your keychain pepper spray unit can be used as an effective striking tool. There are even some pepper spray units designed to be used as a kubotan or yawara stick. Hold it in your fist as normal and strike with the bottom end. Aim for bony, fleshy and sensitive parts such as knuckles, forearms, the bridge of the nose, shins, stomach, solar plexus, spine, ribs, groin, neck and eyes.

Pepper Spray vs. Armed Attackers

Should you use your OC spray when the attacker has a weapon? If the assailant only wants your property, money, jewelry, car, etc., then give it up and don't fight. If they want to relocate you, put you in a vehicle, or restrain you in any way, you must take action, as your chances of survival plummet. Perpetrators are not tying you up for your benefit. They are not taking you to someplace where it will be easier to escape. Your best chance of surviving is to take action now.

Running away, if possible, is recommended, as it is almost always the best choice. Keep in mind; the police hit their targets only one time out of five in actual confrontations. No doubt, the chances that a criminal will hit you are even less. And there's an even smaller chance you'll be hit in a vital area. Of course, all else being equal, wouldn't you rather be shot in a public space than in an empty field somewhere?

In this situation, you'll need to stay calm and avoid any sudden moves. A quick grab for your pepper spray may make the attacker think you're reaching for a weapon, causing them to shoot you. Should you decide to spray the attacker, do it fast and immediately run away. If you're in a confined location, move away quietly making it harder to locate and aim for you.

Defense against a knife (or other edged weapon) attack requires managing the distance between you and the blade. Common sense tells us it is always better to be further from a knife than closer. More space gives you more reaction time. Make use of your environment, maneuvering to get furniture or other obstacles between you and the perpetrator. Keep your attention focused on the attacker's face, you'll still know where the knife is and have a chance to read where he is targeting and what he intends to do next. Never turn your back on a person armed with a knife unless you are more than 20 feet away.

Pepper Spray Tactics at Home and Work

When a criminal breaks into your home you need to assume they are there to commit violence. Most burglars try to be sure a house is empty before making entry. Sure, it is possible that an intruder is just your neighbor's teenage son who had too much to drink. Be aware and alert, but don't make assumptions.

Keeping a larger pepper spray canister next to your bed provides easy access in the event of a nighttime intruder. Keeping pepper sprays in other locations such as by doors and in rooms where you spend a lot of time such as kitchens and TV rooms puts an excellent self defense tool where you can get it without having to fight your way back to your bedroom.

Should you become aware of a home invader do not search for them looking for a confrontation. Stay put in a locked room, call 911, get behind a bed or other barrier, get your pepper spray ready and aimed.

TIP: Also keep a flashlight, a chemical glow-stick attached to an outside door key and charged cell phone near your bed. You can activate the glow-stick and toss it down with your key so the police can get in.

Old cell phones, even without a current service provider, can still be used to call 911 if your landline has been cut. Keep one on a charger concealed in your closet, bathroom or other place of refuge.

Legal Issues

Pepper Spray and the Law

Pepper Spray is legal in all of the 50 states. Do be aware there may be laws about the types, strength and sizes of pepper spray that may be sold or carried. Possession of OC spray may be regulated or prohibited by law in some local jurisdictions. If there is any question in regard to legality, check with local police.

Most state laws require a person be 18 years or older to possess pepper spray. While police may use their discretion and not arrest a 16 or 17 year old who makes appropriate use of OC, they will almost always take action if a minor uses or possesses pepper spray without good reason.

> **TIP:** Never use your pepper spray for any reason except to protect yourself or others from physical harm, sexual assault or abduction! Using pepper spray because someone has been rude, insulting, driving poorly or any reason other than a clear and immediate threat may result in major legal problems.

When traveling outside the United States check the laws of all countries you plan to enter, Most European nations prohibit or strictly limit possession of pepper spray.

Traveling to Mexico while having in your possession a can of pepper spray is legal and it can even be purchased in many Mexican farmicias. However, being in possession of a weapon, even non-lethal ones, while being a foreigner, can bring unwanted attention from the police.

The Canadian Firearms Act of 1995 stipulates that pepper spray is prohibited and illegal within Canada. Pepper spray that is intended for the purpose of injuring, immobilizing or otherwise incapacitating a person is prohibited according to the Canadian Criminal Code. And should you use pepper spray on another person causing serious bodily harm or harming the environment, it can carry a penalty up to a fine of $500,000 and imprisonment of up to 3 years.

But wait, there is a loophole! If the spray is intended (and so labeled) for protection against bears, dogs and other animals it is legal. These sprays tend to be in bigger cans. Certainly, a large can of "bear spray" could provide peace of mind when camping or traveling remote areas. However, carrying it in a populated area without good reason can land you in legal hot water.

You may not take pepper spray onto an airline flight carried on your person or in your carry-on luggage. Amounts under three ounces may be carried in your checked bags. Just to be on the safe side, place your pepper spray in a zip lock bag before putting in your checked luggage.

Where ever you are, if you deploy your pepper spray in self-defense you should always be the first to report it to the police. Be prepared to explain why you believed you were in danger, why you couldn't flee, whether you tried talking the attacker down, getting help, etc.

First Aid for Pepper Spray

If you are sprayed or accidentally spray another we offer this advice.

- DO NOT RUB YOUR EYES!

- DO STAY CALM. Panic makes it worse. Breathe slowly and deeply. **It won't last!**

- Do blow your nose, rinse your mouth, cough and spit. Avoid swallowing.

- Do remove contact lenses or have another remove them, with clean fingers.

- Do treat exposed eyes by rinsing with water.

- Maalox and other aluminum hydroxide or magnesium hydroxide based antacids mixed 50/50 with water to spray on effected areas.

- Do remove your contaminated clothing. In some cases it may make sense to cut off clothing that otherwise would be pulled over the head, possibly adding to the exposure.

- Do wash skin with soap and cool water.

Bibliography

"Evaluation of Pepper Spray"
April 2003, National Institute of Justice
Steven M. Edwards, John Granfield, and Jamie Onnen

"Impact of Oleoresin Capsicum Spray on Respiratory Function in Human Subjects in the Sitting and Prone Maximal Restraint Positions"
May 2000, National Criminal Justice Reference Service USDOJ
Theodore C. Chan M.D.; Gary M. Vilke M.D.; Jack Clausen M.D.; Richard Clark M.D.; Paul

"Joe Rosner's Street Smarts & Self Defense" (dvd)
August 2011, Joe Rosner

"Tactical Use of Defense Spray"
Security Publishing Company
1993, Doug Lamb

"The Effectiveness and Safety of Pepper Spray"
April 2004, National Institute of Justice

"Use of Pepper Spray in Policing: Retrospective Study of Situational Characteristics and Implications for Violent Situations"
Janury 2017, Competency Center South & East, The Swedish Police, Lund University
J. Bertilsson; U. Petersson; P. J. Fredriksson; P. A. Fransson;. Magnusson

About the Author

Joe Rosner became interested in self-defense as a child living in high-crime, gang infested neighborhood in Chicago. In 4th grade h best friend was sexually assaulted by an adult predator on a Saturda morning while on his way to play with Joe. Joe accompanied his friend the police interview and photo array, an experience that left a stro impression. As his family moved frequently, Joe was often subject typical "new kid" confrontations by bullies. He developed humor as way of defusing many of these situations.

As a young adult, he joined the Army and began a more serious study self-defense techniques. After his discharge Joe worked as a bodygua and in law enforcement. He obtained college degrees in L Enforcement and Communications/Mass Media.

His experience in numerous street confrontations and study of mart arts has proved invaluable in developing the ideas and concepts includ in this book. In 2001 he founded Best Defense of Illinois, an organizati that has taught thousands of children and adults how to be safer fr crime and violence. He is a sought after speaker on workplace violen crime safety and self-defense. He has created special programs for r estate, healthcare and other professions.

He can be contacted at: joe.rosner@usa.net

Research in Brief

- In 18 encounters, subjects were not fully "subdued " by OC, in 7 of these incidents, subjects exhibited bizarre behavior and appeared to be on drugs or mentally troubled, thus suggesting that such individuals may not yield to OC's effects.

- While assaults on officers were declining prior to implementation of the OC spray program, the rate of decline increased after OC was introduced.

- Twenty-one officers received minor injuries when they used the spray, but none reported lost work days.

- Similarly, only 14 suspects received injuries, none of which required hospital treatment.

- Use-of-force complaints decreased by 53 percent in the study period despite decreased manpower and increased demand for services. No complaints addressed the use of OC.

- Although training instructions stated that sprays were maximally effective from a distance of 4 to 6 feet, many officers applied the aerosol to humans from distances of less than 3 feet, which may have diminished the spray's effectiveness.

- Overall, study findings showed that a well-developed OC-spray program can provide operational benefits to police.

Target audience: Law enforcement officials and trainers; State, local, and Federal policymakers; researchers.

occur. As an irritant that relies on pain compliance, CN is most effective on those individuals who are lucid and have a normal pain threshold. Individuals who are intoxicated, extremely agitated, or mentally ill generally are less affected by the agent because of their greater tolerance for pain.

Although humans are susceptible to the agent's effects, animals suffer little, if at all, from the symptoms induced by CN. In addition, CN effectiveness is temperature-dependent. While the agent is useful in any temperature over 50° F, it is most effective when used in temperatures of 72° F and higher.

CN use also creates decontamination problems since the microscopic particles can remain airborne for some time after being dispersed. Dissipation time depends on the amount of the agent released, air current activity, temperature, and humidity. Finally, CN cross-contamination between subjects and police officers is common. Officers note that they are often contaminated by the agent when arresting and transporting sprayed subjects. This cross-contamination is thought to be responsible for officers' reluctance to use CN.

- **o-Chlorobenzylidene malononitrile (CS).** CN was replaced as a riot control agent by the U.S. Army and the National Guard around 1960. Officials believed that the replacement, CS, sometimes called super tear gas, was considerably less toxic and delivered more immediate effects than CN. Following military protocols, American law enforcement agencies subsequently adopted CS in 1965. Like CN, it is classified as a solid, not a gas, since it requires a carrying agent to disperse it into the desired target area. CS, a lacrimating irritant, immediately affects the mucous membranes, producing tears, runny nose, and persistent coughing or

sneezing. Additional symptoms of exposure include respiratory distress accompanied by tightness in the chest, a burning sensation on the skin, and nausea or vomiting. In addition to physical effects, CS can also cause intense fear, panic, and cognitive disorientation.

Like CN, CS is more effective on those areas of the skin that are moist and is virtually ineffective on animals. Unlike CN, CS is considered to be effective over a wide temperature range. The microparticulate nature of CS results in agent persistency and thus can make decontamination problematic, especially in enclosed or confined spaces.

Serious injury to an individual is improbable if CS is used properly. Extensive toxicological testing indicates that, in spite of the potency of CS, it is safer, less toxic, and more effective than CN.

- **Oleoresin capsicum (OC).** OC, a naturally occurring substance derived from the cayenne pepper plant, is classified as an inflammatory agent. On contact with OC, the mucous membranes of the eyes, nose, and throat immediately become inflamed and swollen. The symptomatic swelling produces involuntary eye closure due to dilating capillaries; nasal and sinus drainage; constricted airway; and temporary paralysis of the larynx, causing gagging, coughing, and shortness of breath. The extract of peppers causes the blood vessels to dilate and the blood to rush to the upper body; the skin appears inflamed, resembling a burn.

OC's inflammatory properties purportedly render the agent more effective than CN and CS on violent, intoxicated, drugged, and mentally ill individuals. Moreover, the symptomatic eye closure and constriction of the respiratory tract explain why OC is so effective on animals. No special decontamination protocols are required for OC because it is biodegradable. Unlike CN and CS irritants, OC will not persist on clothing or affected areas.

Examination of a national sample of in-custody deaths that occurred subsequent to OC use has excluded the agent as a contributory factor. This analysis concluded that, to date, OC has not caused any deaths.[1] Finally, OC use does not result in dermatitis, skin depigmentation, or burns.

CN and CS are still used by many law enforcement agencies, especially for tactical use in crowd-control situations. Primarily because of the potential risk of injury and cross-contamination, as well as decontamination problems associated with their use, law enforcement officials began to use OC as a less harmful, more dependable alternative. Although available since the mid-1970s, OC was not widely used until recently.

Study method

Research staff adopted a two-pronged approach to the OC spray evaluation task, which they initiated in mid-July 1993. The first phase involved examination of OC adoption and implementation issues. The second stage was concerned with assessing the impact of OC spray in confrontations between police officers and citizens, as well as police officers and dogs.

Phase 1. Officers and command staff members who initiated and were critically involved with the project met throughout the study period to address specific OC-related issues. Research staff attended these meetings and collected information on the process of OC adoption and implementation. Issues in-

cluded selection of the pepper spray product, development of a written policy on its use, development of a training program and materials, implementation of documentation for reporting pepper spray usage, and identification of followup training needs.

Phase 2. Project data were provided by BCoPD's Crime Analysis Unit and Internal Affairs Section, as well as by the monthly *Maryland Law Enforcement Officers Killed or Assaulted* data sheets. This information was supported by data collected from an instrument developed by the research staff to track each spraying incident.

Every officer discharging OC spray in a confrontational encounter was required to complete the OC spray data collection form, which contained both open-ended and specified-choice questions relating to prevailing weather conditions, suspect's behavior, OC application area, injury (if any) received, and decontamination. The OC data form was completed along with a departmental incident report as soon as practical after conclusion of the encounter. A second data collection instrument, an unstructured followup interview, was developed to validate information collected by the OC data form. These unstructured officer interviews were conducted by the onsite observer to allow for the addition of any comments, suggestions, or officer observations regarding the specific encounter and the effectiveness of the spray.

Prior to their use in BCoPD, the OC data collection sheet and unstructured followup interview format were pretested in the Anne Arundel County, Maryland, Police Department. Results indicated that measurement instruments were both suitable and easily completed.

Findings: adoption and implementation

Selection of product. The Baltimore County Police Department had previously undertaken a thorough study of the OC product that it wanted to provide its officers. BCoPD selected a product containing a 5-percent concentration of OC delivered through a fogger system, which does not require precision aiming.

BCoPD training. The Baltimore County Police Department has sole responsibility for delivery of police services to approximately 695,000 people who reside in urban, suburban, and rural settings within its 612 square-mile jurisdiction. Eighty percent of the department's officers are assigned to the Field Operations Bureau, and they responded to 442,436 calls for service in 1993, which included 44,074 Part I offenses. The department needed to train approximately 1,400 officers in a 3-hour block of instruction—without disrupting assignments, affecting manpower, or incurring payment of overtime. To minimize disruption, OC training was incorporated into officer inservice firearms training, which began on July 12, 1993, and continued through December 31, 1993. During this time, 1,345 officers were trained in the use of OC spray and issued canisters.

Standard operating procedures. The BCoPD committee charged with examining the feasibility of OC adoption drafted a Standard Operating Procedure (SOP), following consultation with BCoPD's legal counsel, training officers, Internal Affairs, and command and staff officers. Additional directives were added following the completion of instructor training and writing of the lesson plan. The SOP requires all members of BCoPD whose normal duties include making arrests or supervising arrest situations to carry OC spray. Uniformed members of the department are to carry the device on their gun belts in an issued holster, while nonuniformed officers are to carry pen-sized containers after completing a training program and demonstrating their competence in handling and using the OC spray.

Guidelines for usage. BCoPD, like most other police departments, adheres to the use-of-force continuum and its range of response, beginning with the mere presence of an officer and escalating to the use of deadly force. According to BCoPD procedures, OC spray may be used by an officer in any arrest situation when:

• The aggressor has failed to comply with the officer's verbal instructions.

• The aggressor has been advised of OC's impending use.

• The officer is about to use hands-on tactics to defend himself against active hostile resistance.

• The officer is confronted by an aggressive animal.

BCoPD thus places the use of OC spray above verbal commands on the force continuum as a means of control and restraint. BCoPD emphasizes that OC is not a substitute for a firearm. If, when faced by an armed individual, the officer deems deadly force necessary, then BCoPD considers the firearm to be the weapon of choice.

During the study, patrol officers voiced concern about whether they would be allowed to use deadly force if attacked with OC spray. The Legal Officers Section of the IACP holds that an officer may use deadly force to protect himself from the use or threatened use of OC spray when reasonably sure that deadly force will be used against him

if he becomes incapacitated. Incapacitation includes situations in which officers may be unable to adequately defend themselves due to the effect of chemical sprays. Criteria for determining when to use deadly force incorporated situations in which OC was used against police (see "Reasonable Use of Deadly Force").

The Baltimore County Police Department operating procedures also outlined how to use the product and decontaminate the prisoner after use. The SOP directs officers to assure the suspect of the temporary nature of OC's effects and to provide air and water as first aid. BCoPD officers were instructed to remove the sprayed subject from the spray area into fresh air and to allow access to "copious amounts" of water, as soon as possible. Since BCoPD patrol vehicles did not carry water or any special equipment to aid in the decontamination process, they relied on physically removing suspects, instructing sprayed persons not to rub their eyes, and transporting them quickly to a source of water.

Use of pepper spray

During the study period, Baltimore County officers used OC in response to 194 (174 human and 20 animal) incidents, which fell into various categories of complaints that beat police officers often handle. These types of complaints usually involved aggressive, excitable behavior on the part of both the complainant and victim. Moreover, they tended to escalate quickly, resulting in confrontational outcomes.

Thirty-nine percent of the incidents occurred inside some structure (e.g., house, car), while the remaining incidents occurred "out-of-doors."

Reasonable Use of Deadly Force When Officers Are Attacked With OC

When a criminal attacks an officer with OC spray, he does so with the intent to harm the officer, escape, or both. It is common knowledge that a high percentage of officers who are incapacitated or have had their guns taken away are later shot with their own weapons. To ask an officer to take a chance that the OC spray attacker is going to walk away after incapacitating the officer would be, in the opinion of IACP's Legal Officers Section, unconscionable.

In determining whether an officer's use of deadly force was reasonable, the following factors may be considered:

• The nature of the crime committed by the person or persons confronting the officer.

• The nature of the verbal or physical threats posed by the person confronting the officer.

• The relative strength and fighting skills of the officer and his opponent.

• The number of officers versus the number of potential assailants.

• The nature of weapons in the possession of or available to the assailant.

• The ability to circumvent the potential effects of OC spray.

• The alternative means of defending against the use/effects of OC spray.

• The availability of assistance from other nearby officers.

Exhibit 1. **Force / Threat Used by Suspect**

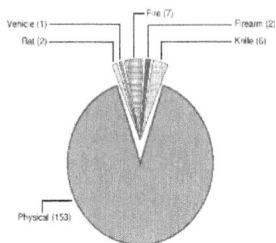

Weather conditions did not seem to influence either an officer's decision to use OC or the spray's effect on suspects. Eighty-four percent of the human subjects sprayed were male and 16 percent were female. Generally, sprayed individuals were intoxicated (drugs or alcohol), belligerent, and/or combative. The majority (89 percent) of incidents involved suspects who physically threatened the police officer; very few incidents involved the use of firearms or knives. The arrest/intervention incidents necessitating the use of the spray were primarily battery, assault, and disorderly conduct (see exhibits 1 and 2).

Effectiveness of OC use

Overall, OC was very effective in the 194 incidents where it was used (see "Officers' Comments on OC" on page 6). A total of 156 (90 percent) of the 174

Exhibit 2. **Initial Contacts**

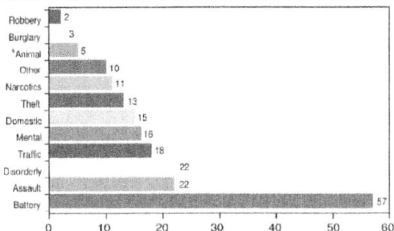

* A total of 20 incidents involved animals, but 15 of these were initially classified (at the time the call was dispatched) in other categories, such as "assault" on police officer.

individuals sprayed were incapacitated enough to be effectively arrested. Data indicate that almost all officers applied OC to the suspect's face, as they had been directed in training. However, officers generally did not spray from a distance of 4 to 6 feet as instructed. In 144 incidents, the spray was activated at a distance of 3 feet or less; in 102 of these, OC was sprayed at a distance of 2 feet or less. As a result, OC may not have been maximally effective.

Yet the data show that OC worked even if it was not sprayed from the distance suggested by the manufacturer. In 144 incidents, only one spray was required to incapacitate a subject; officers used the full contents of an issued container of OC to control suspects in four separate incidents. No data indicated that spraying more than one short burst produced better effects, if the subject were given a "good" spray the first time. The data showed that 117 individuals (67 percent) were classified by officers as submissive after the OC had been applied; 27 individuals (16 percent) were listed as complying with officer instructions after being sprayed (see exhibit 3). The difference between the terms "submissive" and "compliant" is subtle, and it might be more appropriate to collapse the two categories into one. When the categories are collapsed, 144 (83 percent) of the 174 subjects were sufficiently neutralized to yield to officer orders. Thirty individuals (17 percent) struggled or otherwise failed to follow officer instructions.

Eighteen of these 30 struggling subjects were classified by officers as not fully incapacitated by the OC spray. According to officer reports, the OC had no effect on seven suspects. These

Exhibit 3: **Suspect Actions After Application**

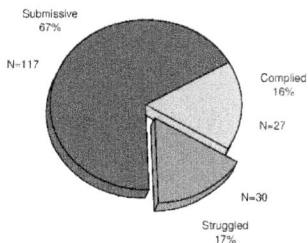

Submissive 67%
N=117

Complied 16%
N=27

N=30

Struggled 17%

Other results of OC use

Assaults on officers. Three years of prior assault data (pre-OC data) were collected for comparison with data from the period after which OC was adopted by the department (post-OC data). The pre-OC data were examined to identify any possible trends regarding assaults. Overall, these data showed that officer assaults were decreasing prior to OC use. The post-OC data indicated that assaults continued to decline. In fact, the total number of officers assaulted in the post-OC period was substantially lower than in any pre-OC data period. While it is likely that the introduction of OC spray contributed to this significant decline, the finding must be considered preliminary, since the pre- and post-data for this study were not strictly comparable in all cases.

Injuries to officers. Data from the spray collection form showed that few officers were injured when they used OC to control a confrontational encounter. Only 21 officers (11 percent) reported receiving any injury (see exhibit 4). Most of these were minor and resulted in no lost work time. Although data from the pre-OC use period were not comparable and did not permit a

seven individuals exhibited drugged behavior or seemed to have emotional problems. These data indicate that individuals who are heavily intoxicated, drugged, or mentally unstable may be resistant or immune to OC's effects or that OC may actually exacerbate the difficulty associated with controlling such persons.[3] Additionally, these types of encounters may cause the officer to be cross-contaminated if the incident escalates to a physical confrontation. BCoPD's experience indicates that training officers may want to stress the importance of accurately assessing the likely impact of pepper spray in such an encounter and of being prepared to select another control alternative.

Animal control. Interest in OC's effectiveness in animal encounters was high because, prior to project implementation, BCoPD had experienced a number of incidents where officers were forced to shoot threatening or attacking dogs. During the OC field study, dogs were sprayed with OC in 20 incidents where the animals posed a danger to officers. Ten of the dogs sprayed weighed between 25 and 50

pounds, and 6 weighed more than 50 pounds.

Data showed that officers sprayed the dogs at distances greater than those from which they sprayed humans. The majority of dogs were sprayed from a distance of 3 to 8 feet, whereas most humans were sprayed from a distance of 1 to 3 feet. The difference in application distances may account for the differences in the effectiveness levels for dogs and humans. OC was effective nearly 100 percent of the time in dog encounters (one officer was bitten but required no medical treatment).

Officers' Comments on OC

The following comments were extracted from the OC data collection sheets completed by the BCoPD officers or from followup interviews:

• Wish we had had it a while ago.

• I think it's a great...alternative to initial use of force.

• Definitely better than using a nightstick.

• The word is out (on the street)...all people have to do is hear the Velcro© and they comply pretty quickly. [The officer who made this comment had actually pulled the OC from his holster at least 10 times, but had sprayed it only once.]

• Some subjects actually apologize after being sprayed.

Exhibit 4: **Officer/Suspect Injuries**

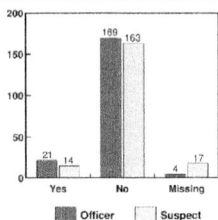

complete before-and-after analysis, the relatively low level of injuries sustained by officers in the post-OC period suggests that OC use has the potential to reduce officer injuries in confrontational situations.

Injuries to suspects. Very few suspect injuries occurred during the post-OC project period. Of the 174 spray incidents, only 14 suspects (8 percent) received any injuries, and all of these were minor, requiring no hospital treatment (see exhibit 4). Staff were not able to gather pre-OC comparison data; however, it was hypothesized that if suspects were injured, complaints of force would be filed more often. The data collected during the study period indicated that such complaints were decreasing at a rate greater than that observed prior to the introduction of OC. It is reasonable to conclude that OC had a positive effect on reducing the number of suspect injuries.

Use-of-force complaints. Departmental policy states that a use-of-force report must be completed if the subject complains of injury as a result of arrest and goes to the hospital for medical treatment. However, as is true for other less-than-lethal weapons, a

use-of-force report is not required for OC, absent a complaint or hospital treatment. BCoPD officials concluded that treating OC differently could inappropriately hinder its use.

Data suggest that despite an increase in calls for service and fewer patrol officers working their beats, use-of-force complaints declined by 53 percent during the second pre-OC period (July 1991 through March 1992) and the post-OC period. Similarly, a reduction of 40 percent occurred between the third pre-OC period (July 1992 through March 1993) and the post-OC period (see exhibit 5). Since no other major policy changes regarding use of force took place during pre- and post-data collection, it is likely that the use of pepper spray accounted for the decrease in complaints. Interviews with Internal Affairs officers add weight to this finding. These officers noted that, unlike those of impact weapons, the effects of OC are short-lived and nontraumatic; pepper spray thus reduces the likelihood that brutality or excessive force complaints would be lodged. In addition, sprayed individu-

als received aftercare from the officers who sprayed them, which may have obviated the need to complain.

During the time of data collection (July 1993 through March 1994) and over the span of 174 sprayings, five complaints of brutality and one use-of-force case were received by BCoPD. These complaints centered on the officer's purportedly inappropriate behavior and did not address the spray itself. To date, BCoPD has not had any complaints or suits filed that relate to the issue of OC spray.

Summary

Most police departments in the United States are concerned about officer and suspect safety. In recent years, this concern has focused on injuries to police officers and citizens during arrest confrontations. To meet this problem, departments have sought answers in technology involving less-than-lethal weapons. Aerosol pepper spray is one weapon from the LTL arsenal that effectively addresses the issue of officer/citizen injury.

Exhibit 5: **Complaints Alleging Force**

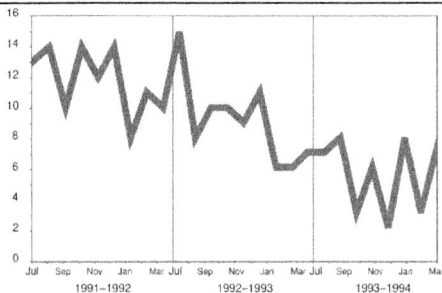

This study's findings indicate that BCoPD successfully implemented its OC operation. Statistical measurements of effectiveness were high, and those related to officer assaults, officer and citizen injuries, and use-of-force complaints were low. Study findings showed that OC spray offers advantages over more problematic sprays and that a well-developed OC spray program can provide a variety of operational benefits for law enforcement agencies. In addition, the process followed by BCoPD could guide other police departments interested in OC implementation.

Notes

1. Granfield, John, Jamie Onnen, and Charles S. Petty, M.D., *Pepper Spray and In-Custody Deaths*, Executive Brief, Alexandria, Virginia: International Association of Chiefs of Police, March 1994.

2. The terms "submissive" and "compliant" were used by officers completing the data collection form. An individual officer's understanding and expectation of OC's effect on a suspect may cause him or her to make a distinction between the terms. Officers who believe that the purpose of OC is to totally incapacitate a subject, with no resistance, might describe the suspect as submissive and conclude, therefore, that the product worked. If the OC did not perform as expected, the same officer might report that the product had no effect—despite the fact that the suspect was easier to arrest as a result of being sprayed. Other officers might believe that the product worked well, even though the suspect offered a struggle. This discussion is offered to caution against strict interpretation of subjective responses.

3. More research is required to obtain definitive answers to the question of how intoxication, drug use, and/or mental illness affect a person's reaction to OC spray.

Findings and conclusions of the research reported here are those of the authors and do not necessarily reflect the official position or policies of the U.S. Department of Justice.

The National Institute of Justice is a component of the Office of Justice Programs, which also includes the Bureau of Justice Assistance, Bureau of Justice Statistics, Office of Juvenile Justice and Delinquency Prevention, and the Office for Victims of Crime.

NCJ 162358

The full report summarized in this Research in Brief was prepared by Steven M. Edwards, John Granfield, and Jamie Onnen under National Institute of Justice grant number 92-IJ-CX-K026. The authors were with the International Association of Chiefs of Police while conducting their evaluation. Questions about the full report may be directed to John Firman, research coordinator, IACP.

U.S. Department of Justice
Office of Justice Programs
National Institute of Justice

Washington, D.C. 20531

Official Business
Penalty for Private Use $300

Appendix II.

U.S. Department of Justice
Office of Justice Programs
National Institute of Justice

APR. 03

NIJ

Research for

WARNING
UNDER
CONTAI
WARNI

The Effectiveness and Safety of Pepper Spray

U.S. Department of Justice
Office of Justice Programs

810 Seventh Street N.W.

Washington, DC 20531

John Ashcroft
Attorney General

Deborah J. Daniels
Assistant Attorney General

Sarah V. Hart
Director, National Institute of Justice

This and other publications and products of
the U.S. Department of Justice, Office of Justice Programs, National Institute of Justice
can be found on the World Wide Web at the
following site:

Office of Justice Programs
National Institute of Justice
http://www.ojp.usdoj.gov/nij

NIJ

APR. 03

The Effectiveness and Safety of Pepper Spray

Comments regarding this
Research for Practice
may be e-mailed to
askost@ojp.usdoj.gov or
sent by postal mail to
LTL Program Manager,
National Institute of Justice,
810 Seventh Street N.W.,
Washington, DC 20531.

To learn more about NIJ's
less-than-lethal research
and development pro-
gram, visit http://www.
ojp.usdoj.gov/nij/
sciencetech/ltl.htm.

Findings and conclusions of the research reported here are those of
the authors and do not reflect the official position or policies of the
U.S. Department of Justice.

The North Carolina study discussed in this report, "An Evaluation of
Oleoresin Capsicum (O.C.) Use by Law Enforcement Agencies: Impact on
Injuries to Officers and Suspects." by J. Michael Bowling and Monica

ABOUT THIS REPORT

This report presents the findings from two recent unpublished NIJ-funded studies that used different methodologies to test pepper spray's safety and effectiveness. One study looked at officer and suspect injuries in three North Carolina police jurisdictions before and after pepper spray was introduced. The other examined the deaths of 63 suspects held in custody after pepper spray was used in their arrest.

What did the researchers find?

- The North Carolina study found that the number of injuries to police officers and suspects declined after pepper spray was introduced. Complaints that the police used excessive force also declined.

- The study of in-custody deaths concluded that pepper spray contributed to death in two of the 63 cases, both involving people with asthma. In the other cases, the researcher concluded that death was caused by the arrestee's drug use, disease, positional asphyxia, or a combination of these factors.

What were the studies' limitations?

- In the North Carolina study, procedures for identifying officer and suspect injuries differed considerably from agency to agency and within each agency over time, which limited the extent of the conclusions that could be drawn.

- The number of in-custody deaths in which pepper spray was used in the arrest process is very low, which makes identification of trends difficult.

- Each arrest situation is unique; it is virtually impossible to collect enough nearly identical arrest scenarios with and without pepper spray in the field to conduct a quantitative study.

Who should read these studies?

Law enforcement policymakers and practitioners, defense and prosecution attorneys involved in pepper spray cases, and medical examiners.

The Effectiveness and Safety of Pepper Spray

Pepper spray, or oleoresin capsicum (OC), is used by law enforcement and corrections agencies across the United States to help subdue and arrest dangerous, combative, violent, or uncooperative subjects in a wide variety of scenarios. Though generally assumed to be safe and effective, the consequences of the use of OC, as with any use of force, can never be predicted with certainty. The need for reassurance on these points remains. This Research for Practice summarizes the results of two unpublished NIJ-funded studies on the safety and effectiveness of pepper spray in real-life arrests and compares them with previous studies. The goal: to expand the scope of knowledge on this complex subject.

One study looked at officer and subject injuries in three North Carolina police jurisdictions before and after pepper spray was introduced. The other examined 63 incidents nationwide in which people were sprayed with OC in the

The North Carolina study found that the number of injuries to police officers and suspects decreased after pepper spray was introduced. Complaints that the police used excessive force also declined.

The study of in-custody deaths, which follows a similar study conducted in 1994,[1] concluded that exposure to pepper spray was a contributing cause of death in 2 of the 63 fatalities, and both cases involved people with asthma. In the other 61 cases, death was judged to have resulted from the arrestee's use of drugs, disease, positional asphyxiation (which may occur when subjects are placed in a prone position, typically handcuffed behind the back, in which breathing becomes more difficult), or a combination of these factors.

These findings complement those of another recent experiment that used healthy volunteers who inhaled pepper spray and were then placed in a sitting position or handcuffed in a prone posi-

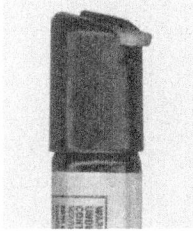

no breathing difficulties in either position.

The North Carolina study

Claims of pepper spray's effectiveness were tested in a 2-year study conducted by a multidisciplinary team of investigators at the University of North Carolina's Injury Prevention Research Center in Chapel Hill, North Carolina. This research sought to assess whether the introduction of pepper spray had reduced the number of—

- Injuries to police officers from assaults.

- Injuries to suspects from police use of force.

- Excessive force complaints against the police.

The records of three North Carolina police departments— the Charlotte-Mecklenburg Police Department (CMPD), the Winston-Salem Police Department (WSPD), and the North Carolina State Highway Patrol (SHP)—were compared for the periods before and after the introduction of pepper spray by each agency. SHP was the first of the three to introduce pepper spray in January 1993. WSPD

and CMPD followed suit in April 1993 and January 1995, respectively.

Data sources

Officer injuries. All information on the use of force by Charlotte-Mecklenburg officers (including injuries to officers and suspects) came from the CMPD Use of Force Database. Information on injuries to Winston-Salem officers and suspects was taken from the Injury Database, 1990–1998. Information on State Highway Patrol officer injuries came from their Worker's Compensation and Medical Only Claims files. Records in which the injury resulted from a motor vehicle crash or actions unrelated to an arrest were excluded. Researchers applied statistical methods to determine whether observed declines in the number of injuries after the introduction of pepper spray were significant enough to be attributed to its use.

Injuries to suspects. Suspect injury data were available from the Charlotte-Mecklenburg and Winston-Salem police departments. No information was available for injuries to suspects

2

arrested by the State Highway Patrol.

Excessive force complaints. Although data on excessive force complaints were collected from all sites, only the State Highway Patrol had data going back far enough to analyze statistically.

Results

Officer injuries. In Charlotte, monthly counts of injured officers declined steadily from 1991 to 1998 (see exhibit 1). This decline began before pepper spray was introduced and continued at roughly the same rate afterward. Before pepper spray was introduced in Winston-Salem, there were two upward trends in monthly counts of officers injured, the first ending in August 1991 and the second in December 1992. After pepper spray was introduced, officer injuries declined, followed by an increase, then a relatively stable period of low counts beginning in December 1995 (see exhibit 2).

Exhibit 1. Charlotte: Officer injuries

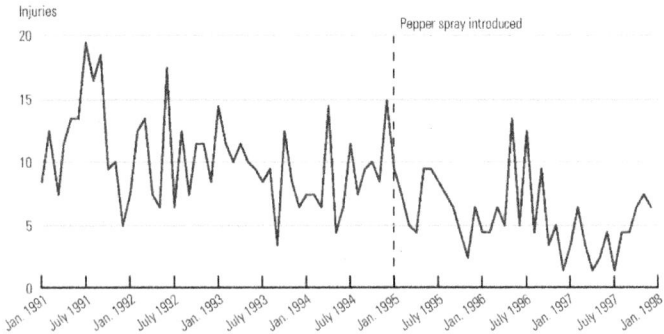

Exhibit 2. Winston-Salem: Officer injuries

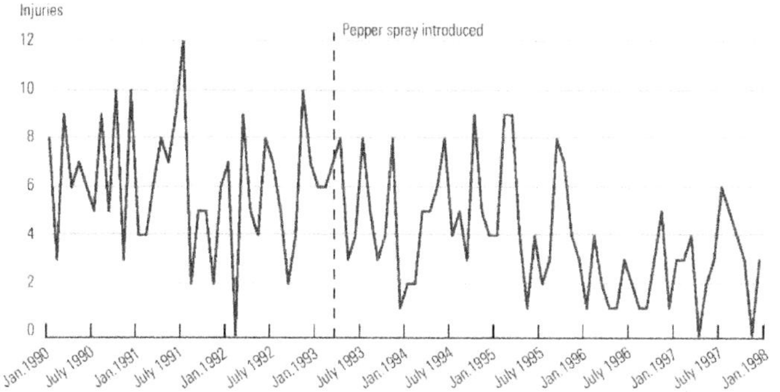

Exhibit 3. State Highway Patrol: Officer injuries

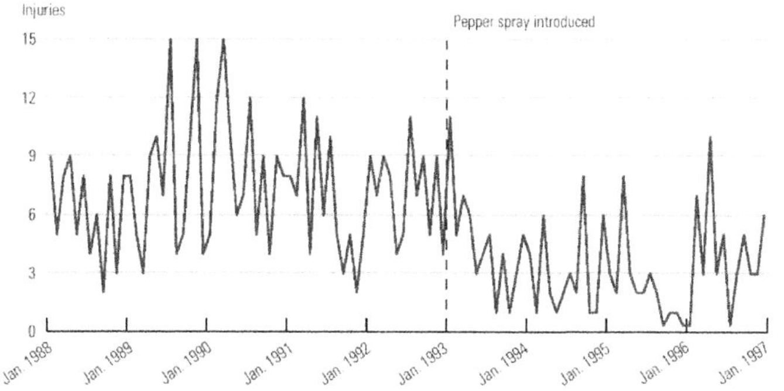

4

The monthly count of injured State Highway Patrol officers, however, shows a substantial decline that corresponds with the implementation of pepper spray. In 1992, 87 officers were injured, whereas only 58 were injured in 1993, a 33-percent decline over a 1-year period (see exhibit 3).

Suspect injuries. Monthly counts of suspects injured by CMPD officers began falling after the introduction of pepper spray (see exhibit 4). In Winston-Salem, on the other hand, monthly counts of

suspects injured by WSPD officers had already been declining before pepper spray was introduced (see exhibit 5).

Excessive force complaints. Ninety-four excessive force complaints were filed against State Highway Patrol officers from 1975 to 1998, peaking in 1992—the year before pepper spray was issued. Complaints dropped sharply after the introduction of pepper spray (see exhibit 6).

Thus, the data suggest relationships between the use of

Exhibit 4. Charlotte: Suspect injuries

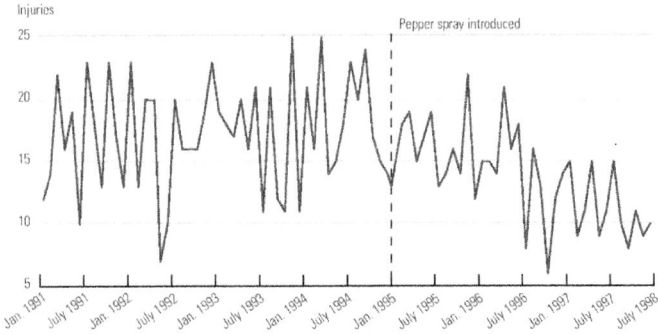

Exhibit 5. Winston-Salem: Suspect injuries

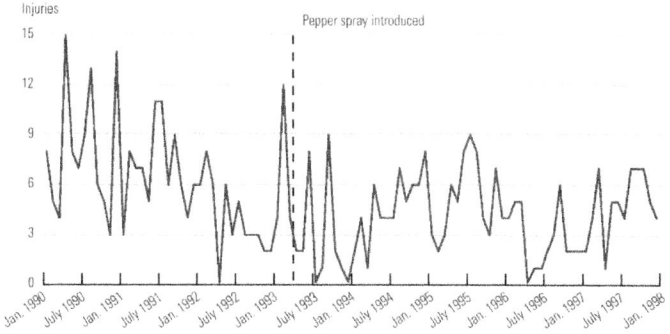

Exhibit 6. State Highway Patrol: Excessive force complaints

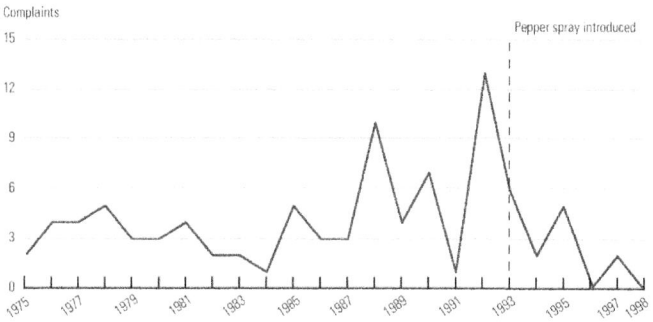

6

pepper spray and declines in the number of State Highway Patrol officer injuries, suspect injuries in Charlotte, and excessive use-of-force complaints against SHP officers. Although pepper spray could have contributed to declines in officer injuries in Charlotte and Winston-Salem and suspect injuries in Winston-Salem, the available data were not sufficient to support those claims. A 1998 study, however, indicated that the introduction of pepper spray reduced the number of assaults on police significantly in the Baltimore County (Maryland) Police Department.[2]

Study limitations. Due to differences among the study's data sources, only a limited number of conclusions could be drawn. The procedure for identifying officer and suspect injuries differed considerably from agency to agency and within each agency over time. The availability of data at each site differed, depending on the level of computer use and the sophistication of programming and software. The systems in place at the State Highway Patrol and in Winston-Salem in the early 1990s required officers to describe the circumstances leading up to injuries. Thus, determination of the number of injuries depended on the officer's recall of the incident and the degree of detail in his narrative report.

Moreover, injuries captured in one system might have been overlooked in others. The State Highway Patrol included only those injuries for which officers had filed Worker's Compensation claims, whereas cases identified in Winston-Salem and Charlotte were not limited to those requiring medical attention or loss of work.

The in-custody deaths study

Early on, as pepper spray use began to spread, questions arose as to its safety, especially after several exposed arrestees died in custody. A professor of forensic sciences and pathology at the University of Texas, Southwestern Medical Center, recently conducted a study of 73 cases of in-custody deaths following pepper spray use to determine the role, if any, played by pepper spray.

7

For each case, the author collected reports from law enforcement sources, emergency medical technicians, emergency room personnel, coroners and medical examiners, and toxicologists. Analysis of police reports of the confrontation was combined with the more quantifiable autopsy findings and, finally, with numerically precise toxicological data. The author believes that information from each of these sources is necessary to have the maximum confidence in the cause of death.

The author did not always agree with the cause of death listed by the autopsy surgeon or medicolegal officer. In some of these cases, he had more or different information than was available to the certifying official at the time an opinion was given on the cause of death.

Classifying the cases

Of the 73 reported cases of in-custody deaths allegedly involving pepper spray, 10 were excluded from the study. Three cases were excluded because investigation showed that pepper spray had not been used. Another seven were excluded because insufficient

details were included in the case reports.

The remaining 63 cases were broken down into four subsets (see exhibit 7):

■ Clear cut—cases in which the cause of death was clear and well-founded.

■ Combined effects—cases in which the cause of death could be attributed to two or more factors working together.

■ Outliers—cases that defied categorization.

■ Asthma—cases in which compromised air passages to the lungs were found at autopsy.

Clear-cut cases. In 12 of the 23 cases included in the clear-cut category, drugs alone were determined to be the cause of death. In another four cases, death was attributed to drugs and heart disease. In the remaining seven cases, the author attributed death to positional asphyxia, which can occur when subjects are placed in a position in which they cannot use the muscles that move air in and out of their lungs. When a subject is made to lie face down, hands cuffed behind, pressure on the abdomen forces the abdominal contents up against the diaphragm, making it harder to breathe. This situation is exacerbated when the subject is obese. Weights applied to the back, such as an arresting officer placing his weight on the subject's shoulder-blade area, also interfere with a suspect's ability to breathe (in one case reported in this study, a sofa was placed on the subject to help control him). Pepper spray was ruled out as a direct or contributing cause in all of these deaths.

Combined effects. In these cases, drugs and disease combined with the confrontational situation to such a degree that it was impossible to isolate a single cause of death. In 23 cases, death was attributed to a combination of the confrontational situation and drugs. In five cases, death was attributed to the confrontational situation and the effects of disease. In another four cases, all three factors contributed to death. Again, pepper spray was ruled out as a cause or contributing factor in these deaths.

Outlier cases. Other weapons or health issues were involved in the deaths

Exhibit 7. In-custody death cases

Category	Number of cases
Category I: Clear cut	23
IA: Drugs alone	12
IB: Drugs and disease	4
IC: Positional asphyxia	7
Category II: Combined effects	32
IIA: Confrontational situation + drugs	23
IIB: Confrontational situation + disease	5
IIC: Confrontational situation + drugs and disease	4
Category III: Outliers (uncategorizable)	6
Category IV: Asthma	2
Total cases examined in study	**63**

and were likely the main cause of death.

Asthma. In the two cases involving asthma, death was attributed to the disease. In one case, details of the confrontation with law enforcement were not available, but the autopsy found signs of preexisting asthma, and the medical examiner certified the death as asthma precipitated by the use of pepper spray. In the other case, signs of asthma were not found, but the autopsy revealed airway damage that could have made the subject susceptible to bronchial spasms triggered by inhaled

9

pepper spray. The autopsy surgeon listed OC and disease as the cause of death.

Pepper spray was used more times in this case than in any other, but according to police officers, it was ineffective. The subject, who was obese, was handcuffed behind his back and placed in a face-down position when being transported. The difficulty of breathing in this position may have been compounded by the damage already done to his airways. In this case, the confrontational situation could have caused or contributed to death.

Was pepper spray the cause of death?

For pepper spray to cause death, it would have to make breathing difficult by closing or narrowing the bronchial tubes. The subject would have to struggle to both inhale and exhale. These effects would be noticeable shortly after the application of pepper spray. Yet, except for the two cases in which the subjects were classified as asthmatics, comments regarding breathing (other than "ceased breathing") were found in only five case reports, none of which referred to a struggle to

breathe. In none of these cases did death immediately follow pepper spray application. For these reasons, the study concluded that pepper spray was not the direct or sole cause of death in these five cases.

Lessons and observations

In addition to concluding that pepper spray did not cause or contribute to death in 61 out of 63 cases, the author viewed pepper spray as a relatively innocuous force option, ranking at the low end of the "escalation of force" scale. Although pepper spray was reported by arresting officers to be effective in only 20 percent of the cases studied, all confrontations examined in the present study were distinguished by the fact that they ended in the subject's death.

A 1999 study that examined 690 incidents of pepper spray use concluded that pepper spray was effective 85 percent of the time, according to the broadest definition of the term "effectiveness."[3] None of the arrestees in these incidents died in custody. Other studies have reported lower and higher effectiveness rates, but effectiveness is a subjective term and its definition varies across studies. The 1999 study found that the effectiveness rate reported by officers was significantly reduced when subjects exposed to pepper spray appeared to be on drugs (about 13 percent of the incidents). In the in-custody death study, toxicological data showed that 39 of 63 subjects (62 percent) had some level of drugs in their body. This apparent large difference in drug use and varying interpretations of what constitutes effectiveness may explain some of the differences in effectiveness rates reported in the two studies.

The current study also concluded that, despite some skepticism as to its existence,[4] positional asphyxia is real and can (and does) cause death. Although pepper spray was not found to be effective in any of the cases of positional asphyxia examined in this study, its precise role in these cases could not be determined. The results of a recent experiment that tested the effect of pepper spray on drug-free, healthy volunteers, by itself and when combined with positional restraint, are discussed below.

Pepper spray and positional restraint

In another study, medical researchers at the University of California–San Diego measured the effects of pepper spray on breathing and other health parameters, particularly when combined with positional restraint.[5] Subjects (34 recruits from a law enforcement training academy) were exposed to pepper spray and a placebo spray and then placed in a sitting position or handcuffed in the "hogtie" or "hobble" position.

The study found that pepper spray inhalation alone does not pose a significant risk for respiratory compromise or asphyxiation, even when combined with positional restraint. Researchers found no evidence that OC exposure resulted in any additional change in respiratory function in the restraint position. In both the OC and placebo groups, pulmonary function was restricted in the restraint position, but measurements remained within the normal range. Moreover, there were no statistical differences between the OC and placebo groups relative to these declines.

11

Pepper spray did, however, result in an increase in blood pressure of 10 to 15 percent, perhaps due to the discomfort and pain associated with it. The clinical implications of this finding are unknown.

This study had several limitations:

- Conditions that occur in the field are impossible to replicate in the laboratory.

- The effects of prolonged sprays and repeated exposures were not studied.

- All of the subjects were cadets at the local police academy and were generally healthy.

- Subjects wore goggles to reduce pepper spray exposure to the eyes, which causes irritation and pain. (The purpose of the study was to measure acute effects of inhalation).

- Restrained subjects were placed on a medical examination table rather than on a hard surface, as often occurs in the field.

- The study did not investigate the long-term effects of pepper spray exposure or the potential for compli-

Practical implications

In-custody deaths occurred before pepper spray was introduced and still occur today in cases not involving pepper spray. Determining the risks of pepper spray in arrest situations is complicated by two facts:

- The number of in-custody deaths in which pepper spray was used in the arrest process is very low.

- Every situation in which a suspect resists arrest is unique; it is impossible to collect enough useful data on nearly identical documented arrest scenarios with and without the use of pepper spray.

The studies cited in this report do not and cannot prove that pepper spray will never be a contributing factor in the death of a subject resisting arrest. In the in-custody death study summarized here, the evidence led the author to believe that, except for two cases, the deaths could be explained as being caused by the struggle with officers and the presence of drugs or alcohol (or both) even if OC had not been used.

The clinical study of subjects exposed to pepper spray and placed under positional restraint, even hogtied, strongly indicates that these conditions alone are unlikely to produce any significant risk to subjects. That study, however, was performed on healthy subjects who were not on drugs or obese. They had not fought with officers or subjected themselves to other physiological or psychological stress that could have compromised their health. These complicating conditions, often found in the field, cannot be replicated in a laboratory. Thus, there can be no definitive clinical determination of the risk of pepper spray use in all arrest circumstances.

The North Carolina study provided results that, in some instances, supported the general belief that the use of pepper spray will reduce injuries to police officers and suspects and excessive force complaints against police. Limitations in the data, however, made it impossible to draw conclusions on all three effectiveness measures at all three study sites.

The in-custody death study noted that pepper spray was reported to be effective in only about 20 percent of the incidents. This rate is much lower than that found in a 1999 study of arrests involving pepper spray, which examined a large number of incidents in which no deaths occurred. The subjects in the in-custody death study had a much higher rate of drug use, however, and there is evidence that pepper spray is less effective on subjects who are on drugs. A possible implication of these observations is that officers may want to move quickly to another force option if subjects appear to be on drugs and seem unaffected by a blast of pepper spray that clearly hit them in the face. Doing so could reduce risks to officers from continually aggressive subjects.

The results of all studies discussed in this Research for Practice seem to confirm that pepper spray is a reasonably safe and effective tool for law enforcement officers to use when confronting uncooperative or combative subjects; they provide no reason to stop using this important less-than-lethal weapon. Other studies continue to be conducted on pepper spray, however, and this will not be the last word on the subject.

13

Additional reading

Kaminski, Robert J., Steven M. Edwards, and James W. Johnson, "Assessing the Incapacitative Effects of Pepper Spray During Resistive Encounters With Police," *Policing: An International Journal of Police Strategies and Management* 22 (1) (1999): 7–29.

Kaminski, Robert J., Steven M. Edwards, and James W. Johnson, "The Deterrent Effects of Oleoresin Capsicum on Assaults Against Police: Testing the Velcro-Effect Hypothesis," *Police Quarterly* 1 (2) (1998): 1–20.

National Law Enforcement Technology Center, "Positional Asphyxia—Sudden Death," *National Law Enforcement Technology Center Bulletin,* Washington, DC: U.S. Department of Justice, National Institute of Justice, June 1995.

Notes

1. Granfield, John, Jami Onnen, and Charles S. Petty, "Pepper Spray and In-Custody Deaths," Executive Brief: Science and Technology, International Association of Chiefs of Police and National Institute of Justice, March 1994.

2. Kaminski, Robert J., Steven M. Edwards, and James W. Johnson, "The Deterrent Effects of Oleoresin Capsicum on Assaults Against Police: Testing the Velcro-Effect Hypothesis," *Police Quarterly* 1 (2) (1998): 1–20.

3. Kaminski, Robert J., Steven M. Edwards, and James W. Johnson, "Assessing the Incapacitative Effects of Pepper Spray During Resistive Encounters With Police," *Policing: An International Journal of Police Strategies and Management* 22 (1) (1999): 7–29.

4. Much of this skepticism resulted from a case in which a forensic pathologist answered that he could not prove, in the case in question, that death resulted from positional asphyxia. (See *Price v. County of San Diego* 990F Supp 130.)

5. More information on this study can be found in Chan, Theodore C., et al., *Pepper Spray's Effects on a Suspect's Ability to Breathe,* Research in Brief, Washington, DC: U.S. Department of Justice, National Institute of Justice, December 2001, NCJ 188069.

14

The National Institute of Justice is the
research, development, and evaluation
agency of the U.S. Department of Justice.
NIJ provides objective, independent,
nonpartisan, evidence-based knowledge
and tools to enhance the administration
of justice and public safety.

NIJ is a component of the Office of Justice
Programs, which also includes the Bureau
of Justice Assistance, the Bureau of Justice
Statistics, the Office of Juvenile Justice
and Delinquency Prevention, and the
Office for Victims of Crime.

Printed in Great Britain
by Amazon